Victoria and Albert Museum

Gaming

The Arts and Living

Edward T Joy

London: Her Majesty's Stationery Office

With the following exception all the objects
illustrated are from the Victoria and Albert
Museum. Fig.25 *Country Life*, displayed in
Astley Hall, Chorley.

Design by HMSO Graphic Design

ISBN 0 11 290301 0

Contents

Figure 1. Modern Thai arrow-shaped cards, as traditionally used in divination.

1 Playing Cards

Playing cards have been in use for a very long time, perhaps as long as a thousand years. Who invented them, and when, is not known, but there are several likely theories and, as so often happens with activities of ancient and obscure origin, unlikely ones; for instance, the charming story of an Indian Maharanee who, irritated by her husband's habit of constantly plucking his beard, devised card games to occupy his hands. Cards were certainly used in their early history for divination in China where they were popular amongst the enclosed women of the Emperor's harem (one Emperor had, in addition to three consorts and nine spouses, no less than one hundred and eight concubines and assistant concubines). These early Chinese cards were probably borrowed from Korea, for they were long and narrow like Korean cards which were themselves probably derived from the arrows used in divination [fig.1]. Another possibility is that Chinese paper money of the T'ang dynasty in the eighth century A.D., which bore pictures of emperors, empresses, provincial governors and notabilities, could have been used in a game. But cards proper, as we know them, appeared about 1120, when fine printing from wood blocks was established. They were certainly being used in India about that time and perhaps European cards arrived from there, for the Indian suit symbols contained cups, swords, rings and sceptres among others, while early European suits were cups, swords, coins and batons [pl.1]. But the exact origin of cards in Europe remains a mystery; perhaps the most acceptable solution is that they developed independently in the East and West.

As to the date when playing cards first appeared in Europe, a monk, Johannes de Basle, writes of cards 'coming to us in this year', viz. 1377. Angelo Covelluzo in the next century maintains that cards were brought to Italy by the Saracens and were used in the game 'naib'. The Arabic word 'nabaa' means 'prophecy' and this supports the theory of their original use for divination. Johannes de Basle also mentions packs of from 52 to 60 cards, apparently in four suits. The earliest known pack made in Europe was produced in Lombardy in the fourteenth century. Charles VI of France bought three packs of cards from a painter, Jacquemin Gringonneur, in 1392. Seventeen cards in the Bibliothèque Nationale, Paris, are thought to be survivors of these. These early cards were 'tarots', 22 in number, used with a pack of 56 in suits as mentioned above, for fortune-telling. They were made of parchment or fabric stiffened with varnish, drawn on or stencilled and coloured by hand. They were always of more value than the cards in the four suits, over which they triumphed (hence 'trumps').

The emblems on these strange cards were usually as follows:

1. Juggler	13. Often unnamed but
2. Popess	meant to be Death
3. Empress	14. Temperance
4. Emperor	15. The Devil
5. Pope	16. House of God or Tower
6. Lovers	17. Star
7. Chariot	18. Noon
8. Justice	19. Sun
9. Hermit	20. Judgement
10. Wheel of Fortune	21. The World
11. Force	Unnumbered – The Fool
12. Hanging Man	*[pl.2]*

Fortune-telling was always frowned upon by the Church and in the latter part of the fifteenth century the game of trumps was denounced for using God, the angels, planets, the cardinal virtues and Pope and Emperor in a game. But the popularity of card games grew rapidly during the fifteenth century and cards were produced in quantity by the use of stencils. The opposition of the Church had little lasting effect and card games spread first throughout Italy, then into France, the Netherlands, Spain and Germany.

Some of the most attractive cards were produced in Germany. Here the suit signs were bells, representing the nobility, hearts, the Church, leaves, the middle classes, and acorns, the peasants *[pl.3]*. Hearts and bells were coloured red, the others green. There was no Queen in these early German packs, the court cards being King, Oberman and Unterman. At Nuremburg in 1390 the first paper mill was set up and soon afterwards cards were made here and printed by wood engraving. This method so speeded up production that by the end of the fifteenth century cards were being exported from Germany in quantity. About 1450 a method of engraving on copper was invented. The cards produced by this means in Germany in the late fifteenth and early sixteenth centuries were among the finest ever made, profusely decorated with natural and other emblems and meticulously coloured *[pl.4]*. Wood engraving continued to be used for cheaper products and different makers employed different suit signs. For example, one had lions, monkeys, peacocks and parrots; another, wine-pots, printers' pads, drinking cups and books. About 1550 the standard of design began to decline.

It was, however, in France that card-playing spread most rapidly, so much so that as early as 1382 it was forbidden at Lille as it was considered to distract men from the practice of archery. Charles VI's early purchases, mentioned above, are recorded in the Royal Treasury accounts of 1392, in which the cards are described as being 'in gold and divers colours,' and made by hand. Cards of this kind were expensive, but the cheaper wood-block method was also employed in France to produce cards in monochrome. Suit signs used in France in the early fifteenth century were coeurs (hearts), trèfles (clubs or acorns), piques (spades, a version of German leaves) and an original emblem for the fourth suit, carreaux (diamonds). The court cards were king, queen and valet (son). About

7

1440 we first find the court cards being named, the valets bearing the names of famous knights. These varied from region to region, local heroes or characters from mythology sometimes being used. In one pack, now in Paris, the kings are Alexander (clubs), Caesar (diamonds), David (spades) and Charlemagne (hearts). It is interesting to note that in modern packs the king of hearts is the only king to wear ermine, a survival of Charlemagne's splendour, while the king of clubs still holds an orb, the symbol of monarchy, recalling Alexander's conquests.

Thiers was the most important centre of paper-making in France and by the sixteenth century the production of playing cards was well established there, with a flourishing export trade *[pl.5]*. Formalised kings and queens decorated the court cards until the Revolution, when philosophers and prominent revolutionaries took their place. Napoleon preferred classical figures, but after his overthrow the old designs returned and are still in use, almost unchanged. Some double-headed cards, as in modern packs, were made in France as early as 1827, but were not in general production until much later.

In Spain, where tarot cards do not appear to have been made, the most popular game was 'hombre' (the man), played with a pack of 40 cards, the eight, nine, and ten in each suit being omitted. Originally for two players, the game was adapted for three, hence the introduction of triangular card tables. It was played in England as ombre, the game which figures prominently in Pope's *The Rape of the Lock*, published in 1714. Other games were 'renegade' and 'la lutte', mentioned in Rabelais' *Gargantua*, 1534. Similar games were played in Portugal, and the voyages of exploration by the Portuguese and Spaniards spread the custom to distant lands. Montezuma is said to have enjoyed watching games of cards and dice. Natives of the Iberian colonies roughly copied the designs of cards on skin or bark and some of these have survived.

Cards came to England in the first half of the fifteenth century, probably from Spain or Italy, or the Netherlands. They were quickly copied and manufactured in England, and the pastime spread, as in other countries, with some speed, for in 1495 it was banned for servants and apprentices except during the Christmas holidays. In December, 1502, Elizabeth of York, Queen of Henry VII, drew one hundred shillings from her Privy Purse for playing cards at Christmas:

'Item to the Quenes grace upon the Feast of Saint Stephen for hure disporte at cardes for Cristmas. C.s.'
(*Privy Purse Expenses of Elizabeth of York*, ed. N. H. Nicolas, 1830.)

Henry VII's losses at cards are recorded in his accounts. Princess Margaret, his daughter, amused herself with cards at stops on the long and tedious journey to Scotland to marry James IV, himself an addict.

During the Commonwealth card-playing was frowned upon because of its association with gambling, but packs intended for education seem to have been permitted, and a set of 'Scholar's Practical Cards' to aid spelling and arithmetic appeared in 1656. Charles II's reign also saw a new departure in cards which commented on current affairs or recent history. These carried illustrations, often with text, over most of the face of the card, a miniature suit sign being in one corner and the number or initial letter of the court card in the opposite corner. In 1680 a pack vilifying Cromwell and his government was published, closely followed by others recording the Popish Plot *[fig.2]* and the Rye House Plot. Later came packs celebrating Marlborough's victories *[fig.3]* and commemorating the South Sea Bubble and other notable events. Other popular subjects were Love Mottoes, Proverbs, Witty Sayings, and Vices and Virtues. In 1797 appeared a charming pack decorated with the Cries of London. In fact, almost any subject could figure on a playing card. The backs of cards were usually plain until Victoria's reign and could be used to write on. John Gay wrote a couplet of the *Beggar's Opera* on the back of the ace of spades and A. M. Toplady wrote the well-known hymn, *Rock of*

Figure 2. The Popish Plot, 1678: Ace of Hearts and Four of Hearts.

Figure 3. Queen of Hearts and Five of Clubs from a pack celebrating Marlborough's victories, 1707–8.

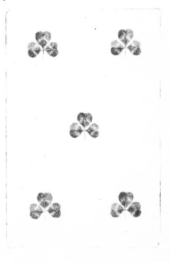

10

Ages (published 1775) on the six of diamonds. A common custom was to give a playing card to a caller at a house who wished to leave a message and from this developed the use of visiting cards, probably after the backs of playing cards began to be covered with patterns in the latter part of the nineteenth century. English cards were outstanding for the beautiful design and colour of the backs.

It was inevitable that the widening scope of subjects would ultimately result in the use of playing cards for educational purposes, as mentioned above, and it was in the seventeenth century that this began. In France Mazarin devised packs to instruct the infant Louis XIV in the elements of geography and history and these subjects were probably the most suitable for this kind of teaching. Packs to teach heraldry were also popular. An early set was published in France in 1655, and one in England in 1675 *[fig.4]*, while in 1684 appeared a set 'The Blazoning of the Ensignes Armorial of the Kingdoms of Scotland, England, France and Ireland and of the

Figure 4. Blome's heraldry pack, 1675: Ace of Clubs and Ace of Hearts.

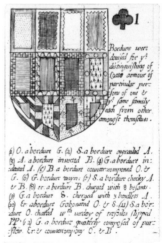

Coats of Arms of the Nobility of Scotland.' This was a fine pack printed from copper plates and coloured by hand, the work of Walter Scott, an Edinburgh goldsmith. Sir Walter Scott, the novelist, is reputed to have owned one of these sets. A pleasant set to teach the geography of England was issued in 1675, each card bearing a map of a part of a county with its principal towns and rivers, its distance from London and other information. The year 1678 saw a more ambitious issue, one to teach world geography; each of the four suits dealt with a continent and the court cards bore portraits of contemporary rulers. The Joker was a cannibal set against the background of the West Indies, described as the Cannibal Islands; the suit of America was clubs, the king being John IV of Portugal with a description of Brazil on his card. Much later, in 1827, another fine similar set appeared, printed from steel plates and coloured by hand, each numeral card carrying a map and the court cards full-length portraits of con-

Figure 5. Reigning Monarchs of France, Prussia, England and Spain. Duty card dates between 1765 and 1776.

Figure 6. Educational cards from Willerton's toy shop, London: Queen Anne as Queen of Spades, Nine of Spades (multiplication table), and Three of Hearts (Ancient Briton). Second half 18th century.

temporary rulers. Geography gave endless scope for illustrations in this way. History was equally popular. Satirical sets to appeal to adults came out from the seventeenth century onwards, but many sets of kings and queens and famous personages were also produced for children [*figs.5 and 6*]. Aesop's *Fables*, 'with fables and morals in verse, to be had of the proprietor, I. Kirk, at the Grotto Toy Shop in St. Paul's Churchyard', were recommended in the *Public Advertiser* of 17 December, 1759. One arithmetical pack carried suit symbols with the king featured as George III, the queen as Queen Charlotte, and the knave as Master Cocker whose popular treatise on arithmetic gave rise to the expression 'according to Cocker'.

The nineteenth century saw a great increase in instruction sets. 'The Royal Historical Game of Cards', issued about 1837, no doubt in celebration of Victoria's accession, illustrated rulers from King John to Queen Victoria. A curious subject for children was 'Trial by Jury' of about 1850, with caricatures of the personnel of the law courts. It was also in this century that many games like 'Happy Families' and 'Snap', which did not employ regular playing cards,

13

made their appearance. They must have brought welcome relief to the over-instructed Victorian young.

There were enough card-makers in London in 1628 to form a company with a royal charter. A duty of five shillings had already been imposed from 1615 (possibly earlier) on every gross of packs imported. The Worshipful Company of Makers of Playing Cards was given power in its charter to seize foreign or defective cards. Two shillings tax had to be paid on each gross of packs manufactured. An Inspector of Playing Cards was appointed by Charles II to collect these fees. In 1710 a tax of sixpence a pack was imposed to pay for the Spanish Succession War, and in 1711 it was decreed that one card in every pack – this was usually the ace of spades – must bear the duty stamp. This tax was altered many times in the next two and a half centuries, rising as government requirements increased, until a decline in sales enforced a reduction. It was finally abolished in 1960.

There were many varieties of card games, each enjoying its period of popularity. Queen Elizabeth I particularly liked the old game of primero. Gleek and Angel-beast were also played during the Tudor period though both games aroused some disapproval; in 1579 Stephen Gosse in *The School of Abuse* writes that 'Dicers and Carders are commonly cried out on.' During the seventeenth century the range of card games widened with triumph, ombre, piquet (imported from France) and écarté (also from France and played with piquet cards in a pack of 36, later reduced to 32). Lanterloo (or, more commonly, loo) and bass t were also fashionable and at this last game Nell Gwynne is said to have lost £5,000 in one night. The prevalence of gaming with cards and dice at the court of Charles II is vividly described in the diary of John Evelyn, who was himself, as he writes, 'no gamester.' On 8 January, 1668 he records: 'I saw deep and prodigious gaming at the Groom-Porter's, vast heaps of gold squandered away in a vain and profuse manner. This I looked on as a horrid vice, and unsuitable in a Christian Court.' The office of Groom-Porter, incidentally, was revived by Charles II for the superintendence of the furniture in the royal apartments, a task which included all the necessary arrangements for the numerous games of cards and dice. When Charles died in 1685, Evelyn writes in his diary on 4 February:

'I can never forget the inexpressible luxury and profaneness, gaming and all dissoluteness, and as it were total forgetfulness of God (it being Sunday evening), which this day se'nnight I was witness of, the King sitting and toying with his concubines, Portsmouth, Cleveland and Mazarine, etc . . . whilst about twenty of the great courtiers and other dissolute persons were at Basset round a large table, a bank of at least 2,000 in gold before them.'

Gleek is mentioned in the diary of Samuel Pepys, Evelyn's contemporary. On 13 January, 1662, Pepys writes: 'My aunt Wight and my wife and I to cards, she teaching me to play at Gleek, which is a pretty game.' Success, with some reservation, is recorded shortly afterwards, on 17 February: 'Going and coming we played at gleek; and I won 9s. 6d. clear, the most that ever I won in my life. I pray God it may not tempt me to play again.'

Another game – whisk or whist – was played in servants' halls during Charles II's reign. Unlike other games, this one rose in the social scale until in 1736 a group of enthusiasts met at the Crown Coffee House, Bedford Row and drew up formal rules [pl.6].

An amusing fad in the nineteenth century was for so-called 'transformation' cards in which the suit signs were made part of the design, though still recognisable as to symbol and number [pl.7 and fig.7]. For instance, the club sign can be found drawn as a negro's head, while spades are part of clothing. W. M. Thackeray, the novelist, designed a set of this type, the three of spades, for instance, being 'Mr. Gibbon, Mr. Boswell and Mr. Johnson', each spade being drawn as a face. Other prominent figures of the period designed these cards, including Dante Gabriel Rossetti and the architect, C. F. A. Voysey.

It is abundantly clear that while all these card games could

Figure 7. Transformation card, French, c.1830. Three of Diamonds as Don Quixote.

be played for amusement only, and one assumes that the educational games were, playing for money or wagers became part of the pastime almost from its inception. Gambling was already rife before the arrival of cards, but their advent opened a new and exciting field to the gamester and now, as skill and not luck alone could sway the outcome, even more people were attracted. Books of advice on gaming were published in the late Stuart period; a later one was dedicated to Sir Isaac Newton in 1718. A few years previously R. Seymour wrote in the *Court Gamester*: 'Gaming is become so much a fashion among the Beau Monde that he who in Company should appear ignorant of the games in Vogue would be reckoned low-bred and hardly fit for conversation.' *The Gamester* was first published in 1674 and was a prolific periodical, giving rules and instructions for many games. In a similar periodical in 1763 appeared the following extract: 'There is a new kind of tutor lately introduced into some families of Fashion in this Kingdom, principally to complete the education of the young ladies, namely a Gaming Master, who attends his hour as regularly as the Music, Dancing and French Master, in order to instruct the young Misses in the Principles of the fashionable accomplishments of Card Playing.' After this it is not surprising to find the very proper young ladies in Jane Austen's novels adept at playing all the fashionable card games for money.

Early in the seventeenth century gaming houses were set up and quickly multiplied to cater for the most popular occupation of the leisured classes. Large sums of money and valuable properties were won and lost and in some curious way the payment of gaming debts became a matter of honour, so that a gentleman would contemplate suicide if he could not meet his losses 'at play' whereas his debts to his tailor, architect and cabinet-maker troubled him not at all. In 1827 William Crockford, the son of a poor fishmonger, opened Crockford's Club in King Street, St. James's for card playing. This Club, which made Crockford's fortune, had the largest gambling room in the world, where enormous sums changed hands. George Smith, the cabinet-maker, whose pattern book, *The Cabinet-Maker's and Upholsterer's Guide* (1828), popularised the late Regency style in furniture, criticised the extravagant neo-rococo furniture in the Club with this acid comment: 'As this mansion is solely appropriated to nightly purposes of pleasure, perhaps such a taste may be in unison with the wasteful transfer of property made in such establishments.'

In spite of Puritan attempts to ban card-playing in the American colonies it survived strongly there, with cards brought from England. Advertisements for English cards appeared for 150 years until the Stamp Act of 1765 which imposed a shilling duty on each pack of cards destined for the American colonies. The Americans imported blocks and began to print their own cards. The first advertisement for vernacular packs appeared in 1790, but imported cards seem to have carried some prestige for a time, for 'London' was

Plate 1. Two circular papier mâché cards. Kashmir, 19th century.

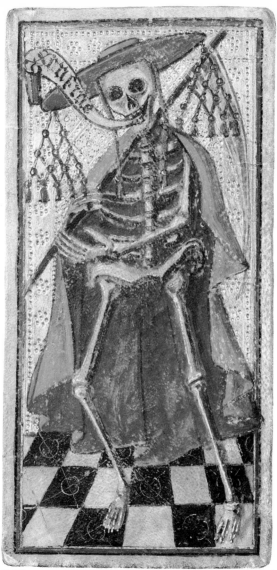

Plate 2. Tarot card: Death wearing a cardinal's hat. Italian, late 15th century.

Plate 3. Knave of Bells. German woodcut, 16th century.

Plate 4. Nine of Rabbits. German engraving, c.1470.

Plate 5. Early French cards, c.1500.

Plate 6 (right). J. Gillray, 'Twopenny Whist', 1796.

sometimes given as place of origin. In 1800 Jazaniah Ford, the first American to be designated a playing card maker, made changes in the design of the court cards, then introduced commemorative packs, the first, probably in 1814, recording the capture of a British frigate during the Anglo-American War of 1812–14. This pack was re-issued in 1824 to mark the visit of Lafayette, with his picture on the ace of spades. J. Y. Humphries printed a pack in which the four kings are pictured as presidents – Washington, Adams, Jefferson and Jackson. Games brought from England – loo, post and pair, whisk and faro – were played in America. Frances Trollope, mother of the novelist, writing in *Domestic Manners of the Americans* (1832), criticised evening parties for being dull, gentlemen playing cards by themselves, 'but if a lady plays it must not be for money.' Some interesting packs were issued during the American Civil War (1861–5). Nelsons of New York produced a Union generals' pack in 1863 and a Confederate generals' pack two years later. At the same time Goodalls of London produced for the American market cards with the backs decorated with the Confederate flag. This practice of issuing patriotic packs in war time has persisted into the present century.

In 1832 the invention of colour printing enabled cards to be run off with greatly increased speed and cheapness; it also led to simplification and uniformity of design. It was no longer profitable to produce small artistic or topical issues. But the backs, previously plain, could now be decorated and in England some outstandingly fine designs were issued [*pl.8*]. Thomas de La Rue was granted letters patent in 1832 for his method of ornamenting cards and his firm paid as much as £30 for a good back design. Three packs designed by Owen Jones, the architect, interior decorator and influential writer on ornament, were entered by this firm at the Great Exhibition, 1851, and earned much praise from Dickens. De La Rue published commemorative packs for Queen Victoria's Jubilees. The corners of cards began to be rounded [*fig.8*] about 1870 and double-ended cards became stan-

24

dard. At the very end of the century cards for the blind, with braille dots, were first made.

In the present century technical advances have enabled cards to be produced in great numbers very rapidly. The faces have become standardised in most countries, but the backs offer a ready field for varieties of pattern and for advertisement. In 1905 the anniversary of Trafalgar was marked in England by an issue of commemorative cards, but contrary to former practice, Nelson's picture appeared only on the backs, and this arrangement seems to be the modern pattern in such packs. There was, however, in the early 1900s an American pack with Presidents for the kings and their First Ladies for queens. As the Presidents' braces were evident in each case these cards became known as the 'President Suspender Deck.' During the First World War several countries brought out packs with heads of state and generals on the court cards. In England Goodalls had drawings by the famous cartoonist Bruce Bairnsfather on an issue. Similarly, in the Second World War a Belgian pack had Churchill as king of spades, Roosevelt as king of diamonds, Stalin as king of hearts and de Gaulle as king of clubs. Hitler appeared as the joker with a bomb aimed at him. In recent years there has been considerable amalgamation of manufactures in Europe and America and designs now seem standardised.

Figure 8. Court card with rounded corners. English, late 19th century.

2 Card Tables

The card tables used by the upper and middle classes rank among the most attractive of the smaller pieces of English furniture. Compact, portable, designed to close or fold up so as to stand against the wall when not in use, they were carefully decorated to take their place in the best rooms of the house. It was not, however, until the late seventeenth century that tables specially designed for cards made their appearance. Previously card games were played on any convenient table or flat surface covered by a cloth which would be removed for board games or dice. 'Tables' mentioned in early accounts refer to backgammon boards. The inventory of the contents of Hardwick Hall drawn up in 1601 mention several times small square tables with their Turkey carpets which almost certainly were used for cards. One such table still at Hardwick, made of walnut, identifiable with an entry in the inventory and dated about 1580, has its top decorated with parquetry which includes playing cards, the five of each suit at the corners.

Naturally enough, these small tables could be used for other purposes as well as gaming [fig.9]. Between 1701 and 1703 Celia Fiennes, in her diary of her travels through England, records her visit to Hampton Court and notes in the 'little anty-roome with presses, a little wanscoate table for tea, cards and writeing.' But by 1700 card tables proper were being made. Surviving examples usually have a circular [fig.10] (more rarely a rectangular) folding top and are decorated with fashionable walnut veneers. They have six legs, two of which are gate-legs which swing out to support the top. These legs often take graceful turned columnar form associated with the reign of William and Mary (1689–1702), though sometimes straight legs of square section are found.

Figure 9. Walnut games and card table. English, late 17th century.

Arabesque marquetry decorates the tops of outstanding examples in imitation of the famous buhl-work decoration in brass, tortoiseshell and other materials which A. C. Boulle made fashionable at the court of Louis XIV. A smaller table was used for the two-handed game of piquet; its usual form was a square top with two flaps supported on a central column with three feet.

The introduction of cabriole legs, of long, slender, slightly curved form, with carved claw-and-ball feet and a carved shell or acanthus on the knees, added much elegance to card tables; convenience, too, for cabrioles did not require the stretchers which restricted players' legs. In the early eighteenth century walnut card tables had rectangular tops hinged

Figure 10. Walnut semicircular card table. English, end of 17th century.

to open out for play. To support the opened top one or two of the cabriole legs, hinged to the framework, were swung out at right angles *[fig.11]*. The tops had rounded corners to hold candlesticks and four sunk wells to take the money or counters. The latter were used by regular, well-to-do gamblers instead of coins. At first it was customary to have small objects such as stones or shells, but by the seventeenth century small discs of token amounts, made of ivory, bone, metal or tortoiseshell, were in use, and occasionally a wealthy player would have special silver or finely engraved mother-of-pearl counters.

To avoid the somewhat ungainly appearance of the single leg swung out to support the top, though this method was to remain in use on card tables during the eighteenth century, some makers adopted the method, from about 1715, of hinging the framework to open out in concertina fashion when one side was pulled back. Walnut remained the most fashionable wood (it was used as a veneer for the table top and frieze and in the solid for the legs) but other woods were also employed. The Museum has a fine example of about 1715 which is decorated with parquetry of laburnum in a striking contrast of colour [pl.9]. With the introduction of mahogany in the late 1720s more carved decoration appeared on card

Figure 11. Walnut card table with raised flap. English, c.1715.

Figure 12. Carved mahogany card table. English, first half 18th century.

tables *[fig.12]*. As was the case with chair legs, a carved lion mask on the knee and carved hairy lion's paw on the foot on each leg of the table became fashionable, giving the name 'lion period' to this phase of early Georgian furniture. Both George II (1727–60) and Queen Caroline were devoted card players, the king's favourite game being commerce while the queen preferred quadrille. In 1737, the year of the queen's death, the Lord Chamberlain's accounts include reference of payment to Benjamin Goodison, the court cabinet-maker, for 'new covering a Quadrille Table with Green Velvet trimmed with Gold Lace and Gilt Nails,' no doubt a reference to one of the queen's tables (PRO LC5/49). No further details are given in this instance, but in 1750 Goodison

30

charged three guineas for supplying the royal family with 'a mahogany Card Table with a folding frame.' (PRO LC9/295) It is most probable that this table was covered with green baize, the usual material for card tables owing to its hard-wearing qualities. The velvet for the quadrille table denotes a piece of exceptionally high standard. At this time some tables had square projecting corners on the tops in place of round ones [*fig.13*]

The Rococo style which reached England from France and became fashionable for some 20 years after about 1740 brought more changes to the form and decoration of card tables [*fig.14*]. This was the age of Chippendale whose designs of Rococo furniture in his pattern book, *The Gentleman and Cabinet-Maker's Director*, have given his name to the anglicised version of the style. Yet, strangely enough, there

Figure 13. Mahogany card table with square corners. English, c.1750.

are no designs for card tables in any of the three editions of the *Director* (1754, 1755, 1762) and it is only recently that any reference was found to such tables in his bills. It is now known that he supplied to Dumfries House, Ayrshire, in 1759:

'A pair of Mahog. Card Tables of fine wood lined wt. superfine green Cloath the knees carv'd & scrol toes to match the chairs.'

These tables and the matching chairs survive in the house and exhibit the characteristic features of the Rococo style, which emphasised C and S scrolls. The table tops are of serpentine shape. The slender cabriole legs end on scrolled feet of French inspiration and their knees are decorated with carved leafy scrolls. The table frames are of concertina type and extend to support the flap when the rear legs are pulled out. Other contemporary card tables exhibit similar features of delicate carved ornament of scrolls, acanthus and shells and of moulded edges to the tops. In the Gothic and Chinese styles which enjoyed a minor vogue at this time, always sub-

Figure 14.
Mahogany card table with Rococo decoration.
English, c.1750.

sidiary to the Rococo, the legs of card tables are straight and are decorated, like the friezes, with delicate lattice-work carving with appropriate Gothic arches or Chinese trellis-work.

So fashionable was card-playing at this time in high society that for a large card party there was often a shortage of tables. To meet the demand cabinet-makers' shops hired out tables for the occasion. In 1763, for instance, William Vile, the celebrated royal cabinet-maker, charged £2 4s. for 'the use and porterage of 4 mah. Card Tables for the Time of the Entertainment of the Venetian Ambassador' in the Prince of Wales's apartments at St. James's Palace.

Most card tables were for four players. For games of two or three players, or a larger number than four, special tables were made: the small table for two-handed piquet, the table with triangular top for three-handed ombre and tredille (the three-handed version of quadrille) and the circular table for loo. Four card tables are illustrated in *The Universal System of Household Furniture*, published between 1758 and 1762 by Chippendale's contemporaries, Ince and Mayhew. Two tables are in full Rococo taste, one is in Gothic; the fourth, 'a traydill table,' has three serpentine shaped sides, pull-out candle stands at each corner, and a carved tripod support.

Perhaps the most elegant of all English card tables were those produced towards the end of the century in the Neo-Classical style made fashionable by Robert Adam. Table legs lost their curved shape. Straight and tapered, square or round in section and ending on spade or plinth feet, they supported tops of various shapes, oval, circular, square or serpentine, decorated with marquetry, painting or carving of light and delicate adaptations of classical husks, honeysuckle, vases, etc *[fig.15]*. In the third edition (1794) of Hepplewhite's *Cabinet-Maker and Upholsterer's Guide*, first published in 1788, the pattern book which set out Neo-Classical designs of furniture for the middle classes, there are two designs for card tables, one semicircular, the other rectangular with serpentine edges, and four designs for inlaid or painted

Figure 15. Semicircular card table in Neo-Classical taste. English, c.1780.

tops. The author's summary is thus:

'Card Tables may be either square, circular or oval; the inner part is lined with green cloth; the fronts may be enriched with inlaid or painted ornament; the tops also admit of great elegance in the same styles.'

This 'great elegance' is also true of the card tables illustrated by Hepplewhite's contemporary, Sheraton, in his *Cabinet-Maker and Upholsterer's Drawing Book*, 1791–4. He shows two designs for card tables with break-front frames, i.e. jutting forwards at the centres and recessed at the corners. He also has three designs for the legs of these tables, 'with stringing and panels let in,' the stringing referring to the delicate

34

inlaid lines which could also simulate panelling in a flush surface, a very popular device at the time.

Contemporary accounts show how gambling at cards affected all classes *[fig.16]*. Charles James Fox had an inveterate passion for gambling. The famous leader of fashion, Georgiana, Duchess of Devonshire, was constantly in debt through her losses at cards. In 1784 she owed £400 to Lady Archer, who kept a faro table, and in 1787 she kept her gambling debts a secret from her husband by borrowing large sums from the banker Thomas Coutts and a further £5,000 from Sir Richard Arkwright, the industrialist and her neighbour in Derbyshire. In his diary Parson Woodforde regularly records the modest sums which he won or lost at whist, loo, quadrille and other games ('At whist this evening lost 0.1.6' – 17 November, 1788). Francis Place, the radical tailor of Charing Cross, draws up a list in his unpublished *Autobiography* (the manuscript is in the British Library) of his acquaintants, often men with good businesses, who became destitute through gambling at cards in the numerous

Figure 16. Cards and dancing; G. Cruikshank's 'A Long Headed Assembly', 1806.

taverns, alehouses and clubs in late eighteenth-century London.

The circular tables for the round game of loo, which had no limit to the number of players, were often of substantial size and were popular because they were so useful for other purposes than cards. In *Pride and Prejudice* (1811) Jane Austen describes how Elizabeth Bennet on entering the drawing-room at Netherfield 'found the whole party at loo and was immediately invited to join them, but suspecting them to be playing high, she declined' and retired to read her book. Her preference for reading astonished Mr. Hurst, 'an indolent man, who lived only to eat, drink and play cards.' The next evening the loo table did not appear; instead, 'Mr. Hurst and Mr. Bingley were at piquet.'

By the early nineteenth century loo tables of the larger kind had a massive central support of a pillar or a triangular pedestal on a base with three or four feet, a form which was to continue in the Victorian period. About 1845 Holland and Sons of Mount Street, London supplied the Queen's Drawing Room at the newly-built Osborne House (where it remains today) with 'A fine satinwood and gold loo table with shaped and carved pillar and angle base, 4 ft. 6 ins. diameter' at a cost of £46 14s. The Museum has an example of the smaller type of loo table of about 1850, made of mahogany with its glazed top inset with metal plaques. Papier mâché loo tables, inlaid with mother-of-pearl, were also popular about the mid-century.

A favourite form of Victorian card table for four players had usually a rectangular top which was made to swivel round and open out on the frame. This method gave the top a firm support and obviated the need to swing out a leg. The space between the top and the frame acted as a drawer to keep the packs of cards.

3 Board Games

Board games have been played from ancient times, not originally on a board but probably on squares scratched in the dust with pebbles for pieces. Such a game, 'patteia', was played by shepherds in Asia in pre-Homeric times and is said to have whiled away the tedious hours for the Greeks at the siege of Troy. Monarchs, of course, amused themselves with more elaborate objects. A splendid set of board and pieces, the largest of three such sets, was found in Tutankhamen's tomb, the ivory board, marked out in 30 squares, forming the lid of an ebony box decorated with gold [pl.10]. The 'men' are of ebony and ivory. The moves seem to have been controlled by a die of small sticks. The game was called 'senet' and resembled modern snakes and ladders. Herodotus and Plutarch mention dice and draughts in ancient Greece, and dice of the Roman period have survived. In the ruins of Pompeii gaming tables have been found marked with 36 squares. Scores have been found scratched on paving stones and columns, and the discovery of a loaded dice demonstrates that more than amusement probably depended on such games.

Among old board games we can certainly include backgammon, for a triptych found at Pompeii shows two men playing the game in a tavern, quarrelling over the moves and, in the third section, being evicted. Backgammon has been played in almost every civilisation of the past, simulating racing, unlike chess which simulates war. Chess was unknown in the ancient classical world and its origin is uncertain. Its most likely ancestor was a game played in Persia ('chaturanga') in which moves of elephants, horses, chariots and men were decided by throws of dice. The earliest documentary evidence appears at the beginning of the seventh century A.D. in several areas, all in Persia or North-West India, at about the same time. Tradition in those regions favours India as the originator. The pieces in the Indian game *[pl.11]*, as set out for play on a board of 64 squares, were, and still are, foot soldiers in a row in front of the major pieces, chariots in the corner squares (the horse moving in the same way as the knight in modern European chess), elephants in the third squares from the corners, and king and counsellor in the two central squares. The oldest legend about the invention of chess goes back to pre-Islamic times and tells how Queen Hasinga of Persia sent her son to quell a rebellion in which he was killed. No one wished to break the news to her, so the philosopher Qaftan was consulted, and after three days' concentration he directed the making of chessmen from black and white wood and of a board covered with leather and marked out in 64 squares. On this he devised a game to simulate a battle. He invited the Queen to play and when the king was in check said 'Shah mat' (meaning that the king was confined or overcome). From this the Queen understood that her son was dead.

The game took an extraordinary hold in Islamic countries where it developed with many complex rules and strategies. From the Middle East it reached Europe in the eleventh century. At first the old game was played but after about 1500 changes were made and the game became more sophisticated, so that modern chess as played in Europe is very different from the Islamic original, though enough similarity in rules and language remains to confirm a common origin.

An examination of the names of chessmen gives us a clue to their evolution. The Arabic 'shah' or ruler becomes the European king. The Arabic 'firz', a wise man or counsellor, has become the queen. This transformation has been a gradual one. 'Firz' was not understood and was rendered in most European languages by a feminine noun, becoming in Middle English 'fers'. Ultimately, because of its position on the board next to the king *[fig.17]*, this piece developed into the queen as this seemed the most likely character. The

Figure 17. Chess-piece, probably a king. Walrus ivory, English, second half 13th century.

Arabic 'fil', the elephant, has undergone a similar complete change in European chess. The elephant was unknown in European warfare and this piece has taken diverse forms, the bishop in England, for example, the count in Germany and the fool in France – all indicating how little the original chessman was understood. On the other hand, the Arabic 'faras', the horse, has become the European horseman, readily identified with the feudal knight *[fig.18]*. The Arabic 'rukh' or chariot explains the use of the word 'rook' throughout Europe for the piece which is also known in England as the castle *[fig.19]*. In some European countries the rook is represented by a wheel, and in Russia by a boat. Finally, the Arabic 'baidaq', or foot soldier, has become the Latin *pedo*, the Spanish *peon*, and thus in English the pawn.

The first known mention of chess in Europe is in the will of Count Ermangard of Urgel in 1010. Cardinal Petrus Damiani, in a letter to the Pope written between 1061 and 1062, condemns the clergy, and in particular a bishop, for taking part in lay sports, among which he includes chess. But despite such criticisms, chess became very popular throughout Europe. Before 1100 there are very few references to the

39

game in surviving documents, but in the twelfth century fifty such references are recorded in England and France alone and over a hundred in the following century. By 1250 the Church had relaxed its strictures against the game so much favoured by the ruling classes; it was now played in monasteries and had spread to the wealthier burgesses and merchants. Troubadours carried a chess set as well as their musical instruments in order to amuse their patrons.

In England King Canute (1016–35) is said to have quarrelled over a game of chess with Earl Ulf as a result of which

Figure 18. Chess-piece, knight on horseback. German, 16th century.

Figure 19. Chesspiece, rook or castle. Walrus ivory, English, 13th century.

the Earl was slain on the King's orders. Canute is also said to have made a gift of crystal chessmen to Hyde Abbey, Winchester. Though these references are of doubtful authenticity there are numerous records in the early Middle Ages of gifts of crystal chessmen to churches. These were probably cut up later to enrich vessels and book bindings and other objects of veneration.

The celebrated Paston Letters, which give us such an illuminating picture of life in a country house in Norfolk in fifteenth-century England, provide interesting details of the domestic games played at the time. Margery Paston writes in 1484 to her husband concerning her enquiries about the 'sports' which were permitted at Christmas in Lady Morley's family, then in mourning. The reply of Lady Morley is thus summarised:

'. . . there were none Disguisings, nor Harping, nor Luting, nor none loud Disports; but playing at the Tables and Chess and Cards; such disports she gave her Folks leave to play and none other.'

Knowledge of chess was an important part of the education of a nobleman's children, girls as well as boys, for skill in play

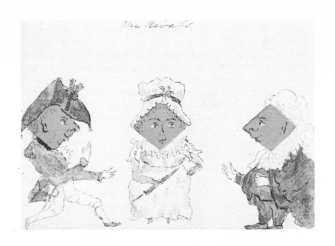

Plate 7. Transformation cards: Nine of Spades and Three of Diamonds. Woodcut, ink and water colour. English, c.1820.

Plate 8. Design for a playing card by C. F. A. Voysey (1857–1941).

Plate 9 (right). Card table decorated with laburnum parquetry. English, c.1715.

Plate 10. Gaming ('senet') board from Tutankhamen's tomb. Ebony and ivory.

44

Plate 11. Chessmen, carved ivory painted and gilt. Indian, c.1800, showing troops of the period.

46

was considered a necessary accomplishment [*fig.20*]. It was permissible for a man to visit a lady in her chamber to play chess, a privilege which became a useful aid to courtship, as many medieval romances show. Chess was the only game at that time which demanded much mental concentration and its reputation was no doubt enhanced when William Caxton printed his illustrated *The Game and Playe of the Chesse* in Bruges, probably in 1475, and again in London about 1480.

Chess now spread downwards from the nobility in the social scale. In some indentures apprentices were forbidden to play at chess or tables. Universities generally forbade chess and games of chance together with jousting, hunting and hawking. Sometimes when chess was permitted it was on condition that the stakes were limited. It seems unlikely that the game would have reached the peasantry, though George Owen in his *Description of Pembrokeshire* (1603) declares that

Figure 20. The Game of Chess. Italian ladies at play. Engraving after Anguisciola, c.1550.

Il giuoco di Scacchi

in Whitchurch 'in ancient times the meanest and simplest of people, yea the plain ploughmen, were skilful at chess play.' There is reason to believe that the game was played in taverns, where the sign of 'The Chequers' may have indicated that chess could be played, though the reference may have been to draughts.

As the medieval period came to a close, however, chess was no longer the only intellectual pastime available for amusement. Games of a less serious nature and shorter duration were needed. In the fifteenth century cards made their appearance and offered a tempting variety of more exciting games, suited to the gambling that was endemic in court life. Towards the end of the fifteenth century the moves in chess were changed and the game gained in variety thus off-setting for a time the change to card-playing, but by the eighteenth century cards had become very much the typical pastime of the upper classes and chess had lost its hold.

The designs of chess pieces have very diverse origins. Indian pieces are of two types, those in which the animals and men are represented in miniature and those of abstract shape which were cheap to make and were consequently more widely used. Mohammedans are forbidden by their religion to make representations of living creatures and thus chessmen from Islamic countries are always abstract in form. In Burma, of Buddhist faith, on the other hand, the chessmen are pleasing little life-like figures. Still further East, in China and Korea, the game is played differently; the pieces move along the lines and not on the squares, while in Japan, pieces captured from an opponent can be added to a player's army. These pieces are simple counters with their names inscribed. In China elaborately carved chess sets, almost all of Indian ivory, were specially made for the European market. The most superior kind were of solid ivory mounted on heavy carved octagonal bases. They were stronger than those mounted on concentric balls, though these were by far the most numerous.

No reference to chess can ever exclude the Russians, whose

great skill at the game is patent today. In seventeenth-century Russia the Czars kept special craftsmen ('shakhmatiks', from shakhmate, the Russian word for chess) to make and repair chess sets. Inventories of this period list sets of crystal, amber, stone and ivory in the imperial possession. Such sets were common Easter offerings to the Czar. A Muscovite embassy to Louis XIV was said by the French to excel the best players in their country. Russian skill at chess was confirmed by an English visitor to Russia in 1772, as recorded in Twiss's *Chess* (1789):

'chess is so common in Russia that during our continuance at Moscow I scarcely entered into any company where parties were not engaged in that diversion; and very frequently I observed in my passage through the streets the tradesmen and common people playing it before the doors of their shops or houses. The Russians are deemed great proficients in chess.'

In European Russia the rook takes the form of a boat, as it does also in Siam, Bengal and Java. One explanation for this is that in the sixteenth century the boat and sledge were the normal means of transport in Russia, so that the chariot would be meaningless.

So popular was chess in medieval and Tudor times in England that cooks sometimes created sweetmeats in the form of chessmen on a board. Such a dish featured in a banquet given by Cardinal Wolsey at Hampton Court in 1528 to the French Ambassador, a compliment to a nation also renowned for its skill at the game. 'And because the French Men are very expert at that Sport, my Lord Cardinal gave that same to a French Gentleman, commanding that he should be made a good Case to convey the same into his Country' (Anon., *Memoirs of the Great Favourite Cardinal Woolsey*, 1706). Chessmen, usually rooks, also feature in heraldry, particularly in the arms of families with 'rook' or 'roc' in their names (e.g. Rooke, Rookwood, Rocold). The heraldic form is normally that of two wing-like projections on the base of a chess-piece.

Throughout Europe chessmen were made in a great variety of forms which were influenced by national traditions. Many different materials were used, including wood, ceramics, ivory, bone, glass, cast iron and, only rarely, silver. There were, in addition, thousands of ivory sets imported from China [fig.21]. In England many notable ceramic sets were produced by Wedgwood in the 1780s and later to the designs of John Flaxman, for whom the famous actor and actress, Charles Kemble and his sister, Mrs. Siddons, are said to have sat as models for the kings and queens. In the early nineteenth century English turned bone and ivory sets were made by a few craftsmen among whom Charles Hastilow, who exhibited at the 1851 Exhibition, was outstanding.

Figure 21. Chessmen, carved ivory. Chinese, 19th century.

Figure 22. Three pawns, jasper ware. English, modelled by John Flaxman in 1785.

Standardisation of form of chessmen became essential when international chess competitions were inaugurated, for players naturally disliked playing with unfamiliar sets. England played a leading part in achieving a common standard, for in 1835 a set designed by Nathaniel Cook and taken up by Howard Staunton quickly gained international acceptance. Staunton was the most famous English chess player of the nineteenth century. In 1843 he became unofficial champion of Europe by defeating the French master, Saint-Amant in Paris in a match for £100 a side.

After more than a century Staunton chessmen remain standard throughout the world. Simple symbolic forms are used, mounted on plain turned stems on firm bases – a crown, coronet, mitre, horse's head (adapted from the Elgin Marbles) and castellated tower serve for the king, queen, bishop, knight and rook, while a ball on circular discs serves for the pawn.

Chess boards were, of course, equally suitable for draughts, of which mention has already been made. The game of draughts (also known as 'checkers') is, like so many others, of ancient and obscure origin and, because of its simpler rules, may well have preceded chess. It was certainly known in ancient Egypt, Greece and Rome. In about the twelfth century A.D. its early form was adapted to the 64-square chess board and by the sixteenth century the modern game in its essentials had emerged. The first recorded book on draughts was published in 1547 in Spain where the pastime may have arrived from Arab sources via the Moors, formerly the occupying power. In England the pioneer work on draughts was published in 1756 by the mathematician, William Payne, with a dedication by Doctor Johnson who was very fond of the game. By 1900 draughts had become so popular throughout the world that very many books had already been issued on the subject. The game achieved international status in 1904 with a representative match between Great Britain and the United States.

Figure 23. Board game and pieces in box, believed to have been made for the Prince of Wales (later Edward VII), c.1850.

4 Backgammon and Chess Tables

The popular medieval games of chance, chess, backgammon and dice, were played on boards which were set upon convenient pieces of furniture. 'A pair of tables' was the medieval term for two boards hinged together and opened out for play. This double-hinged arrangement probably explains why 'tables' became the accepted name for backgammon (which was also known as 'tric-trac'), and 'tables' in this sense is the term used by both Chaucer and Shakespeare. In August, 1502, the Privy Purse accounts of the Queen, Elizabeth of York, record the sum of ten shillings 'delivered to the Quenes grace at Tabuls' by her gentlewoman, Elizabeth Lee, this sum being the Queen's winnings at backgammon. But 'tables' could also refer to the chess board, and some costly examples of these, obviously elaborately decorated, are included, with their chessmen, among the possessions of Henry VIII, Katherine of Aragon and Charles I. It is clear that the decoration included precious metals, rare woods, ivory and other expensive materials.

The chess board in the now familiar form of squares inlaid on the top was established in the eighteenth century and was often incorporated in small tables.

The Victorian love of novelties is seen in some of the chess tables on show at the Great Exhibition, 1851. Jennens and Bettridge of Birmingham exhibited a 'multum in uno' papier mâché loo table which could be used for chess, draughts, bagatelle and other games. John Webb, the royal cabinet-maker of Bond Street, exhibited a carved walnut chess table in Gothic style with the squares marked out in Minton tiles. Another exhibit, by Elizabeth Rose of Oxford, was a screen, embossed on both sides, which was convertible into a chess table.

A small and very useful piece of furniture which neatly brought working and leisure facilities together was the lady's

Figure 24. Work and games table, rosewood. English, c.1820.

combined work and games table, basically a small table with a lifting top covering a receptacle for needlework, usually a silk bag or pouch (hence the name 'pouch table' which was applied to these pieces). This special table did not appear until the second half of the eighteenth century when it immediately established itself as a firm favourite and continued to remain so throughout the nineteenth century *[fig.24]*.

Cabinet-makers of the Hepplewhite and Sheraton eras delighted in ingenious fitments on small pieces of furniture, and the work tables, always light enough for a lady to lift or to move about easily on its castors, were soon provided with an adjustable fire screen at the back and with various flaps or slides for writing, reading and games. Chess and backgammon boards were the commonest kinds. They were often fitted as slides beneath the top, or sometimes the table top itself, which served also as a writing surface, could slide out and be reversed to show a chess board.

Sheraton's *Cabinet Dictionary* (1803) illustrates two examples. One has a chess board top, the other a hinged top which folds over to reveal a backgammon board. Cabinetmakers competed with each other to provide work-and-games tables with the most fitments. In 1811, for instance, Ackermann's *Repository of Arts*, a journal devoted to the latest fashions, illustrates a lady's work table by the well-known firm of Morgan and Sanders with 'seven different accommodations.' The furniture pattern books of the early nineteenth century, the commercial designs of the mid-century of such firms as William Smee and Sons, and the later commercial catalogues rarely fail to include examples of these combined tables. They generally conform to prevailing decorative fashions, but in the revival of Georgian styles which occurred towards the end of the Victorian period, there was a return to the simpler forms of the Sheraton period. C. and R. Light, for example, one of the largest wholesale furniture firms of the time, illustrate tables in their catalogues from 1881 onwards which differ little from those which were in fashion almost a century before.

5 Shovel-boards

A game of considerable age which is still played is that of shovel- or shuffle-board. Strictly, the board of this name is a long narrow table marked by thin lines across its smooth polished top, sometimes with shallow receptacles or nets at the end. The game was played by driving coins or flat discs of wood or metal from the edge of the table with a blow from the palm of the hand so that they could slide along the top into one of the marked sections. This game, which began life as a pastime of the upper classes and gentry, is better known today as shove-halfpenny and is a familiar sight in working men's clubs and public houses, though it no longer requires the long table.

The game is known to have been invented in the fifteenth century and soon became popular in great houses, where the shovel-board was a prominent piece of furniture. Henry VIII was fond of the game and his Privy Purse expenses of 1523 mention the sum of nine pounds paid out to cover his losses. Contemporary references in the seventeenth century clearly illustrate how widely the game was played. Players carried round with them their special coins known as 'shovel-boards' (the same name as the game itself) or 'shovel-groats.' Two of Shakespeare's plays written about 1600 mention these. In *The Merry Wives of Windsor*, Slender complains that he has been robbed of 'two Edward shovel-boards' which had cost him two shillings and two pence each. In *Henry IV*, *Part 2*, Falstaff urges 'Quoit him down, Bardolph, like a shove-groat shilling.' Like so many other popular pastimes, shovel-board was frowned upon during the Protectorate. The old royal palace of Ludlow Castle had a special 'Shovell-Board Room', the contents of which were sold by the Cromwellian government after Charles I's execution in 1649. But inevitably the

Figure 25. Oak shovel board. English, c.1665.

game sprang to life again after the Restoration of Charles II in 1660. In 1662 John Evelyn in his *Sylva*, a masterly study of timbers, describes elm as the best wood for 'shovel-board tables of great length.' Indeed, no other piece of furniture specially designed for domestic pastimes has matched the length of these tables. Among surviving examples the best known is probably that at Astley Hall, Chorley, Leicestershire, an Elizabethan house reconstructed in 1665-6 [*fig.25*].

The table, standing in the hall added to the house at the time of this rebuilding, is 23 feet 6 inches long and stands on 20 ring-turned baluster legs with massive cross-stretchers and a central linking stretcher. Its frieze is decorated with pierced carving. A receptacle ('swallowing dish'), in shape like an empty drawer, is fixed to one end of the table to catch the coins and discs. This table is made of oak but its top is covered with thin boards of parquetry decoration to provide a smooth surface.

Pepys gives us an illustration of the growing appeal of shovel-board in an entry in his diary for 30 July, 1662. Engaged with Sir William Batten in a survey of shipping, he arrives at Woolwich expecting to meet him – 'but he is not come, so we got a dish of steaks at the White Hart while his clerks and others were feasting of it in the best room of the House and after dinner playing at shuffle-board. God help the King! What surveys shall be taken after this manner!'

In the eighteenth century the game lost its aristocratic connections and became the humble pastime familiar today. Small shovel-boards with divisions marked on top were used, or else servants in large houses naturally took advantage of the large tables often found in their quarters to play the game in whatever leisure time was available to them. At Ickworth, Suffolk, a large elm table, formerly in the servants' hall, is marked at one end with the appropriate divisions. This table was used by the male servants; the women's table, of similar length, is not marked for the game.

6 Billiard Tables

The game of billiards was known in England in the sixteenth century, probably introduced from France where it had been played in the previous century. The green cloth on billiard tables is said to represent grass, for the game is reputed to have first been played in the open air on a smooth lawn. Shakespeare mentions the game in *Antony and Cleopatra*, written about 1606–7, when Cleopatra says to Charmian, 'Let's to billiards,' though this, of course is antedating the game by many centuries. Few early billiard tables have survived as they have been replaced by improved versions. The earliest tables had a square top with a single hole in the middle, but during the seventeenth century the modern form of a rectangular top with four corner and two side pockets with nets was established. The Museum has an early example of a table of this form of about 1660. It is made of oak and pine and has six spiral-turned legs. It stands 3 feet high, and is 12 feet 2 inches long and 6 feet 2 inches wide. Its present top, of mahogany, is a later addition *[fig.26]*.

References in seventeenth-century literature show that the game was very popular; indeed, Cotton's *Complete Gamester*, 1674, states that there were few English towns of note without a public billiard table. Pepys records several times in his diary playing the game. On 14 August, 1665, for instance, he writes: 'After dinner, beat Captain Cocke at billiards, won about 8 shillings of him and my Lord Berouncker.' Many large houses had billiard rooms. Celia Fiennes, in her visit in 1697 to Euston, Suffolk, the home of the Duke of Grafton, saw in the Long Gallery 'a square in ye middle where stands a billiard table.' Robert Howlett's *The School of Recreation*, 1684, sets out the formal rules of the game and gives a very detailed description of the

Figure 26. Billiard table, oak and pine. English, late 17th century.

construction of tables, stressing the need for careful framing of the tops to prevent warping.

During the eighteenth century, when the present double square proportions of the top became standardised, the great skill required in the manufacture of billiard tables made this a highly specialised craft – 'generally a branch of itself,' as Sheraton wrote in his *Cabinet Dictionary*, 1803. Gillows of Lancaster and London were particularly well known in this branch of the furniture trade for their improvements in design. Another specialist firm were Seddons of London. In his *Memoirs* William Hickey records his pleasure at acquiring in Calcutta in 1791 'a very capital billiard table made by Seddons . . . at the price of one thousand sicca rupees.'

Designs for billiard tables do not appear in the furniture pattern books of Chippendale, Hepplewhite and Sheraton, though the latter makes a passing reference to them. It was long thought that Chippendale did not make such tables but recently discovered bills show that he supplied Paxton House, Berwick-on-Tweed, in 1774 with 'a large size mahogany Billiard Table lined with superfine green cloath with mace, balls and other materialls' for £37 10s. The mace, used instead of a cue, consisted of an oblong 'shoe' or block of wood, slightly curved, attached to a long thin tapering handle.

Chippendale was also almost certainly the supplier, again in the 1770s, of a 'writing, Billiard and Trou Madame table (in one)' to Appuldurcombe House, Isle of Wight. Unfortunately neither of the Chippendale tables has survived; the combined writing and games table would have been of particular interest, trou or troll madame being the old name of the game played by ladies and resembling bagatelle *[fig.27]*.

The game of billiards became progressively popular during the nineteenth century. A billiard room was accounted a status symbol in the houses of the prosperous middle classes. Later in the century in working class areas of the towns 'temperance billiard halls' proliferated. The game retained its hold on the upper classes. Prince Albert was a devotee and a table at Osborne made by the firm of Thurston of London has colourful decoration carried out under the Prince's direction. Thurstons were probably the most famous makers of billiard tables of the century and were pioneers in one of the most important constructional improvements, that of substituting slate tops for wood.

Figure 27. Walnut bagatelle table. English, c.1850.

Bibliography

Beal, G. *Playing Cards and their Story*, 1975.

Carter, T. F., *The Invention of Printing in China*, 1925.

Hargrave, C. P. *A History of Playing Cards* and a *Bibliography of Cards and Gaming*, 1966.

Hicklin, F. *Playing Cards* (Victoria and Albert Museum Small Colour Book 12), 1976.

Hoffmann, L. (ed.), *Hoyle's Games Modernized*, 1903.

Liddell, D. M., *Chessmen*, 1938.

Mackett-Beeson, A. E. J., *Chessmen*, 1968.

Mann, S., *Collecting Playing Cards*, 1966.

Metropolitan Museum of Art, New York, *Chess, East and West, Past and Present; a Selection from the G. A. Pfeiffer Collection* (Exhibition Catalogue), 1968.

Morley, H. T., *Old and Curious Playing Cards*, 1931.

Murray, H. J. R., *A History of Chess*, 1913; new edition 1962.

Murray, H. J. R., *A History of Board Games other than Chess*, 1952.

Tilley, R., *Playing Cards*, 1967.

Tilley, R., *A History of Playing Cards*, 1973.

Van Autenboer, E. *The Turnhout Playing Card Industry, 1826–1976.* 1977.

Whiting, J. R. S., *A Handful of History*, 1978.

Index

Printed in England for Her Majesty's Stationery Office by McCorquodale Printers Ltd, London
Dd 596344   C50